TASTES
OF
HONEY

Tastes of Honey

A collection of song lyrics, poems, prose, and proverbs "wisdomisms" by Grammy award winning songwriter Ric Marlow

Cover design by Jonathon Eller and production assistant Kristine Krall.

(This has only taken 53 years to put together.)

TASTES OF HONEY

ISBN 978-1-908191-21-2 (ebook)
ISBN 978-1-908191-17-5 (Paperback)

Escargot Books and Music
Ojai, California

This book is dedicated to those who know the
difference between:
"I love you... I want you... I need you..."
and
"I love you... What do you want?... What do you Need?"

and to Julia, who showed me.

I think I've lost my place in time,
for here I am, a man of rhyme,
who whiles away the idle hours,
spouting lyrics to the flowers,
watching clouds go drifting by ...
thinking thoughts of love, not hate;
not too stupid, not too great. Not
too skilled at magic art, playing
life as just a part,
spinning through each lifetime maze,
in search of purple passion days.

Many passions
Many lives
Many lovers
Many wives
Did I learn anything yet?

CONTENTS

LOOKING

Wisdomisms

To fly like an eagle on
the wings of a dove
is man's most ambitious dream.

Force is man's greatest perversion.

Life's moment is but a temporary gift
We are obligated to life to seek out the beauty it
affords us.

Life's prize is Life's game –
How we take that journey is what matters.

We move through each lifetime
to its end – and on and on –
The journey is the destination.

Prelude

All the lost were lonely,
waiting, listening for a sound,
searching for a sign,
hoping for the magic power
that transcends the dust
to heaven's hour.
Going separate and alone,
never caring, never daring.
Lonely wanderers,
desperate in their final hours,
trying to find the way.
They were living in a fog,
a misty mazed bog
of damp desire ...
spurned and scorned
by Summer's fire,
embers of love's funeral pyre,
glowing lower,
never higher.
They were living in a dream.
of nowhere places,
nothing faces,
mindless, kindless,
human races worn
out by
life's empty chases ...
and they heard a voice say

Continued...

"*If you come with me*
you will wander through the rainbow's golden glow,
and bathe, forevermore
in rippling streams of
Love's eternal laughter"

I travel a road of love, peace, and pleasure.
There is nothing to fear on that road.

Come with me

Come with me.
Let your heart be free.
Sailing the shining sea
on silver wings.

Hand in hand, through
tomorrow's land, we will
walk with love, and hear
her sing ...

There's a stream
of forgotten dreams,
and a mountain green,
with emerald spring ...

Love waits there,
like a lady fair.
We will linger
in the laughter
of her afterglow,
this I know,
Come With Me......

(Used by Hawaii Visitor's Center as a promotion to help
entice visitors to the islands.)

We fear no fear of evil here.
We taste no tears of sorrow.
We linger on the shaded brink of time,
that life can borrow,
from some unreal, unraptured, imaged placelet,
called tomorrow.

Don't Ask Me For Tomorrow

I cannot even promise you today,
so please,
do not ask me for tomorrow.
Time is One ... it's
just that way,
so the now should be
for laughter,
and if there is
an after,
then that's the place to
worry about sorrow.

So let me hold you
in my arms,
and let me touch you
while we last,
and we'll never need
the future,
and we'll never miss
the past,
and everything we do
will be
forever and a day,
and where we are together now
is where we'll always stay,
but I cannot even promise you today.

Wisdomisms

When does man realize his destiny?
The day he lets the wind move him
and does not try to stop it or change it.
An impossible task? Almost.
No fear - no danger - no enemy - no stranger.

For the time-
The time for-
Time for the-
To the time-
Drink to the time-
Wine for the time-
For the time, wine-
The time wine, for-
Time, wine for the-

As I sit here in time,
And listen to the wind chimes song-
Am I still a prisoner of the past, So
far, the only thing to last?

Time, - Time - Time
The tool that mortars use to tell eternity by.
Time is nothing to the sea:
She doesn't count the seconds that it takes for her to
be,
nor does the rippling stream recall the
time it takes to become a waterfall.
And trees grow tall in morning and in afternoon
and the sun knows not the numbers
of the hours that it slumbers.

Time, - Time - Time
Man has always tried to tame it,
but the best he did was name it.

The Question

Where does it blow, that lovers wind
that whispers in my ear at night,
and sings a song of rare delight?
A glowing soul
to fill the empty spaces of desire,
and light my way through time,
and give me life eternal
for just a little while?
Where is her smile?

Where is the wind
that blows a lover's mist across my eyes,
and touches with her lips
the unknown land?

Where is the wind that whispers
like a sigh across my eyes,
and touches with her mouth
the empty place in time?
When does she blow?
When does she come? When
will I hear her chime?

Blue October Morning

Maybe on some blue October morning, I'll
see the summer sunlight on your hair.
Maybe in a deep December daydream,
a breath of you will whisper through the air ...
Maybe on some red September sunset,
or a golden August afternoon,
I'll listen to a silver throated wind chime,
and hear the faintest echo of your tune.
Maybe on some amber autumn evening,
a blush of you will linger in the skies.

Maybe in some winter coated canyon,
I'll find the hidden rainbows of your eyes.
Maybe on some blue October morning, I'll
wander like an April foolish moon, into
some misty, half-forgotten garden,
and hear the faintest echo of your tune ...

and when I hear the song you sing,
I'll think of some forgotten spring,
and know my heart will be reborn,
maybe on some blue October morn ...

FINDING

Have you come to teach me now
of love and all its gentle ways,
and change the pounding passion
of another time to days
of tenderness and reason, with
your laugh that shines forever
throughout every season?

The Find

I see your face glowing
with the radiance of a
thousand sunrises.
Warm and brown and velvet is your wind,
as your whisper in my ear.
I feel your soft greedy mouth
drinking from my lips. Who
are you?
Why do you come to me?
Why can I see you,
but I don't know who you are?
Have I just touched you once,
or are you all the lovers I have ever known?

*I offer only
what is mine to give,
A love to last
long after we are gone,
A secret, haven heart,
where we will live
forever,
in a never ending dawn.*

When all the other singers
and their songs,
have been and gone, then
I will sing for you ... a
simple song or two,
about the way I feel
each time I look at you.

When all the other poets
and their poems,
are memories past, then
I will write for you a
simple poem or two,
about the way I feel
each time you make me new.

If you've heard my song before,
I'll be on my way,
but, if you'd like to hear some more,
perhaps I'll stay,
and fight your way
to the long-forgotten feelings
in the world today.

It Was There

I have lived in yet another place,
a stop in time where no one else has been,
and it was there I knew your other face,
your face of love no other eyes have seen.

I have watched an unborn flower grow,
in some unseeded garden yet to be,
and it was there I learned to love you so,
and you, forever, loved another me.

I have touched the rainbow's crest
of blazing gold,
and held a wisp of moonlight ribbon
in my hand,
and sipped, from your warm, velvet mouth,
a kiss that ne'er grew cold.
and it was in the yesterday
of sweet tomorrow's land.

Yes, I have been where yet no one has gone,
and I have lived what yet there is to be,
and in that place,
through love's eternal dawn,
yours is yet the only face I see ...

And who am I who talks of love to you

Am I some wise man, wandering the land?
Or am I but a gust of wind,
blowing o'er the fiery sea,
holding out an empty dream
in my empty hand?

Today I might just be a wanderer,
and tomorrow I might be a king,
then, I may fly like the wind in the night,
in search of a new song to sing,
But I will follow my heart as it wanders
through all of its changes of mind, and I
will drink all the wine
that life squanders,
and leave my tomorrows behind...

But who are you who asks how love will be?
Are you a seeker, hungering for life?
Or are you but a frightened child;
searching for your loaf of bread, and
finding it, your hunger stiff, afraid
to touch the knife ???

Follow Your Heart

Follow your heart
to a valley where love surrounds you.
Don't be afraid
of all that life can be.

When winter rainbows
fill your eyes,
you'll remember
Summer's ember.

Deep in the night,
the song of the wind
in her flight,
whispering,
"love is waiting
for the taking."
Open your eyes
to the wonder of spring
around you;
taste all the joy
that only love can bring.
A magic somewhere
waits for you,
Follow your heart ...

Wisdomisms

Trust your lust if trust you must.

The true master
is the stave
who is blindly obedient
to his own desire ...

Love is just around the corner of your smile,
Hidden in the hallway of your eyes,
cradled in the comfort of your warm and tender
arms,
sheltered in the music of your sighs.

A loving hand?
More--- Understand the
who I am, And what, and
why,
And love me more
For that you see
That says of it
It's time for Thee ...

ENJOYING

My Bell, My Song

*There's a song in my heart that keeps trying to sing
to me,
a longing from deep in my soul.
There's a bell here inside that keeps trying to ring
to me,
and tell me that love is the goal
When I look in your eyes, and I see that you love me,
I can fly ... I'm an eagle ... I'm strong,
And I know by the stars and the heavens above me,
that YOU are the bell and the song.*

*I was down on the ground with no one to desire me,
And nothing inspired my soul.
Then you came, and you found me, and started the
fire,
that is burning beyond my control,
and I knew all at once that I'd love you forever,
even though they all said it was wrong.
I was right... they were blind... and we're here together
And YOU are my bell and my song.*

*So come on and ring to me, sing to me,
songs that will cling to me, always, wherever I go ...
In the mountains, and valleys,*

Continued...

on life's lonely highways,
on rivers of love's melting snow,
in the darkness of evening,
the shadows of morning, through
autumn and winter to spring, you will
always be here,
with your voice loud and clear, and
YOU'LL be the song that I sing.

For the rest of my life I will keep you inside of me,
And sing you, whenever I choose,
And when trouble and strife try to strip off the hide of me,
your laughter will chase out the blues.
I will stand in the sunlight of your lovely melody,
and nothing will ever go wrong,
and I know, that in spite of the Heaven. And Hell in me,
I finally heard what the music's been telling me,
that YOU are the song, baby YOU are the bell in me.
And YOU are MY bell and MY song.

Beautiful Lady

Beautiful Lady,
My heart belongs to you
I'll sing my songs to you, forever ...

Beautiful Lady,
the promise in your eyes
takes me to paradise,
let's fly together.

Come into my arms,
and fill my heart
with sweet and tender passion ...

Touch me with your smile so warm,
a smile that only love can fashion.

Beautiful Lady,
this was worth waiting for,
you are a woman now
a child. no more,
and here am I, at Heaven's door,
about to reach my star,

Oh, Beautiful Lady, How
beautiful you are ...

Irene's Song

I don't have to climb the highest mountain
And I don't have to swim the deepest sea, And
I never have to try to be some other guy, All
I've got to be for her is me.

I don't have to have a million dollars,
She wouldn't care if we ever had a cent.
She just looks into my eyes,
And I own paradise,
even when I haven't got the rent.

She doesn't know of jealousy,
Or foolish insecurity,
Because her love
won't let those feelings in.

She loves me like the child she is.
And all of her is all she gives,
and she gives it to me-
time and time and time again.

I don't have to think about tomorrow.
she fills today with all there is to be.
And I never have to lie,
or try to reach the sky,
All I've got to be for her is me ...

Continued...

She doesn't ask me where I've been,
She's happy that I'm home again,
Whenever I've been gone
a little too long.

She's gentle as a summer breeze, she
loves to love, she loves to please,
and she pleases like the lyric
of a lovely song.

Hanky Panky Lady

She was tall, lean and lanky.
She never got too cranky.
She fovea to hanky panky all night long.

She could do it in the morning
long before the day was dawning
and when the nighttime came
she still was coming on.

She's a lover, she's a lady. Even
though her past is shady .
And you could say she knows her way around.. But
she set my soul on fire and filled me with desire and
always got me higher — never brought me down.

Hanky panky lady, she still drives me crazy.
Even though it's years since she's been gone.
I still want to hold her — I remember what I told her.
She can come back anytime she wants.

I love you
For the strength you give me,
Because you need it...
For your faith...
For knowing...
For loving...
For making me your hero...
For the reality...
For giving me the time...

Wake up with desire, baby,
Coming from your soul.
Smile and greet the morning part
That makes your half a whole.
Fill me with the feeling
That you missed me all night long.

Wake from sleep, my beauty queen,
To things you only think you've seen,
To greener valleys, bluer skies,
Higher mountains, lover's eyes,
To hands that hide a gentle touch,
Yet yearn to share it very much.
With your desire, need and lust,
That says: "I love you, and I trust."

And I will wander aimlessly
Beside you on forever's highway,
My goal to share
All that makes you beautiful.

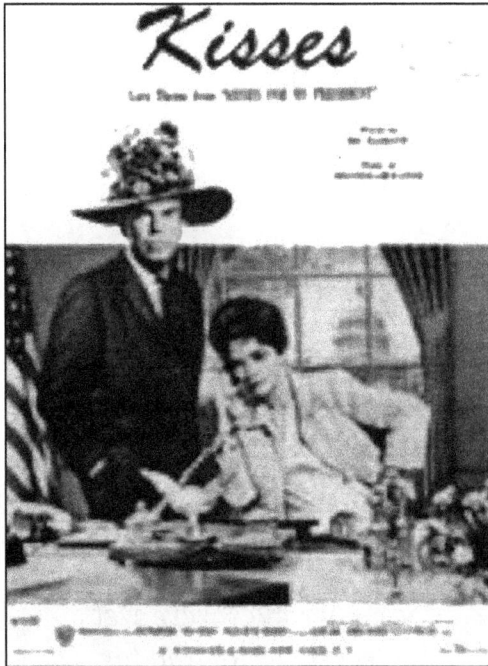

Kisses fan the flames of love, melt your heart away,
Kisses plan the games of love any lips can play,
Suddenly she's oh so near, whispers apart-
There goes your heart.
Yearning for her, burning for her tender kisses
that will tempt and tease 'til they drive you wild
Feel that trembling in your knees, you're like a child.
you're bewitched and in a spell you can't resist.
Now you know the wonder of how two lovers fall in love
and you know it starts with just one kiss.

Her mouth was hungry
feeding fire to her face.
Her cheeks were blazing
with desire,
and her eyes were wet
electric, yearning for
the flame.

You came into my life, and gave me life...   You
took me from my hell, and gave me peace...
You touched me with your need for love,
of which I had the need to give...
You let me taste the joys of some sweet other time
that I had long forgotten.
You let me feast upon the now of some sweet time
I'd never known, and when I had feasted
you said to me
"Let me go....
set me free"
So must I love you more for this?
You opened up the dam, and let my river flow,
and then, when you had bathed in me
you said it's time to go.

You said someday I'd understand the greatness of
our love,
You said another form will come to take my body's
place in
your embrace, and you will capture him
as you did me, and you wire love him
because he's there...
But he will never know the sweetness that I feel,
each time I reach into my soul
and feel my love, without the
chains and binding. You said
someday I'd understand but you
didn't tell me when.

Love Please Tell Me

Love, please tell me, what's the reason
your heart changes, like the season,
cold as snow in winter weather,
warm as spring, when we're together,
changing colors in the fall,
I sometimes wonder if you're real at all?

I can't understand your madness,
first you fill my heart with gladness,
then you change my joy to sorrow,
what will you be like tomorrow?
Will I feel the summer glow?
I wonder how your fickle wind will blow.

Will the breeze be warm,
as warm and gentle as your lips can be?
Will I feel the chill,
the chill of autumn when you look at me?
Will I be left alone and lonely
in the winter rain,
or will I see the blush of spring
upon your face again?
Love, you've got to make your mind up,
just how you and I will wind up,
hand in hand down some sweet lane,
or on separate paths again?
You know how it has to be.
So love, please tell me now, and set me free....

Wisdomisms

Love...
You have to earn it to get it.
You have to give it to keep it...

Love's moment is eternal,
savor it, flavor it with honeyed kisses.
Sip slowly from her cup.
Only a fool has eternity in his hands
and loses it to impatience.

Love is not measured by the amount of pain
you are willing to endure for it,
but by the amount of pleasure it brings.

Oh fickle heart how
fair you flourish in
indecision's arms...

Beliefs, like people, change as life goes on.
Be not confused by these changes... accept
them as the truth of the moment... the
moment of truth...

LOSING

Solitude is always not a lonely place,
'tis there I see, more oft than here,
a smile upon your face,
in your eyes there is no sorrow,
only tears of golden rain
that trickle like a mountain stream
slowly down your cheek, and there is
no need to speak.
Then suddenly, the violent wind,
that is your winter, blows from
under summer's glow,
and the smile that was my sunlight
fades, like melting, steaming snow,
and the angry wind that's cold and mean,
that stashes things it's never seen, drives
me out to seek a fairer clime,
a gentler breeze, a smoother sea, and
drifts me down to heaven's land,
where once again the sky is fair,
and love and I embrace each other
and remember not the angry days,
but live again in love's sweet time
and only you and I are there....

I see the lonely winter in your eyes,
where once, the summer danced, like silver wind.
upon the emerald rain-dropped pools of your desire.

I see the gentle sorrow on your face,
where once, the sun did shine and blind
the darkness from this darkened place.

I see the longing deep within your soul
to touch a star, and race the moon on
comet tails of blazing gold.

I see the yearning deep within your heart
to not grow old without a love
to warm the frozen time when life stands cold.

I see the simple hunger to be free,
a child of space and time, sailing
on your velvet cloud above the
hungry sea

Sometimes a ruthless spirit
stalks the gentle soul
provoking it to madness...
relentlessly pursuing the tenderness
with brash demand...

Love tires
running from the distance
in your eyes.
Love expires when
it tries to hide in
some disguise.

I stand and listen to the rolling tide
and waves that break in whispered sounds,
almost like kissing.
The wind is cool across my chest,
and you are warm and peacefully at rest.
I move inside to find a robe, and warm again,
I stop and gaze upon your face, your eyes,
closed in sweet surrender.
I kiss you silently, with my heart,
hoping not to awaken your body from its peaceful
dream,
but wanting to embrace your soul
with all the passion of my being,
and I feel old, and sad, and tired.
Have I just taken from you all these years?
Have I been just a fool in wise disguise?
And every time I looked behind the tears,
have I not seen the love light in your eyes?

Forgive me love, for I have done you wrong.
I cannot bear to take away your youth, or
make you old too long before your time. I
really meant to be a better man,
but something always happens to the plan,
I only hope there's time to try again
to find that meadowland where we belong,
that space in our togetherness
that we both long to share.
We must be more than just a stop in time. Now,

Continued...

*once again, I weep those bitter tears of youth, and
try to see, through tear filled eyes,
what truth there is for me.
Is this the answer to the question now?
I seek the answer I'm afraid to know,
Is love the holding on, or letting go?*

A lover's laughter... after...
the sound of music.
A lover's sigh... goodbye...
the sound of music.
A lover's lie...
the sound of sadness.

Every Time

Every time we listened to the music, Love,
I thought that we were hearing the same song...
I guess, at times, you really tried to tell me that
we were out of tempo
and the tune I heard was wrong...

Every time I thought we danced together, Love,
I guess I should have listened to your heart...
I would have heard the beating
of another kind of drummer,
and we might be together now, instead of years apart.

Every time we looked into each other's eyes,
I could have sworn that we both saw the light.
I must have been a foolish child,
or else I would have known,
that you were looking at the sun
and I was blinded by the light...

Every time I had my arms around you, Love,
I thought your heart was locked in my embrace.
I guess if I had looked a little closer,
I would have seen a stranger in your face .

And now it doesn't happen for us anymore,
I need no words to tell me you are gone.
you're living in the afternoon of your new love affair,
and here am I still waiting for the new dawn...

There was starlight in the meadow,
and the sunlight cast a shadow,
and the lovelight slowly faded from the dream.
We were only in the morning
of a lovely crystal dawning,
and we waded through a never ending stream.

There were roads we should have wandered,
there are things we should have done, now
the time we had is squandered,
and we cannot find the sun.

The rain has come upon us, and there's winter in the
land.
The summer breeze that used to warm us,
has a damp chill in her bones...
The palms move restlessly in the wind,
then calm, still, nothing for a moment,
then stop, a place to catch your breath.
The ocean recedes passively. Take
me to the desert deep inside,
where I can warm my soul,
alongside desire's fire.
Let the smell of your warm perfumed spirit
drift upon my senses.
Let me wander in the valleys of your love forever.

To sit in silent sorrow, and
never speak the words that
bring today to life,
is wasting not today alone,
but just as well, tomorrow.

And so we turn away from now,
and put our faith in when
and die a little every time we do
and I will miss you.

The flicker of the flame,
beginning or just dying,
seems to be the same, but
we were laughing then
not crying....

The moment now has passed,
but it will last forever
in my eyes....

There's something to be said
for standing in the rain,
and watching someone go,
and feeling half again,
There's something to be said.
for tears that cannot speak,
but hide behind your glasses
and tremble down your cheek.

There's something to be said for
all the morning laughter, for
the days we chased the sun, but
I think, still ever after,
of the deeds we've left undone.
The rhymes unrhymed,
the words unsaid,
and all the songs unsung.

A summer breeze,
a scarlet sky,
the blush of wonder
in her eye.

A velvet glow,
a sudden rain
that lover's cry
of silent pain.

A brief embrace,
the lifetimes pass,
and all there is,
is in the glass...

I sit and wait for you, dear world,
to tumble down around my head.
The timing gone,
the wisdom dead,
the sweet fulfillment
still unfed,
the question's answer
still unread,
and what is here
is in its stead....
a real illusion....

Whatever became of the beautiful child
with the candle light eyes,
and the soft, gentle face?
What pseudo-hiptarian
sits in her place?

Whatever became of that make believe girl,
with the rain forest hair,
and the warm tender hand?
What out of tune tooteress
now leads the band?

Will you really let me go
to wander through the world
So empty and alone,
in spite of what we've known?

Will you forget my face,
and never speak my name,
except, perhaps, in dreams
of love's enchanted place,
and life's forgotten schemes?

Prisoner of the past,
how long will it last?
How long before I find another you?

Tonight, in a cozy place, where we once sat,
I sat alone, and drank the bitter wine of solitude.
I sipped from the glass, and tasted your tears...
Bitter, yet velvet soft... warmly intoxicating.
I breathed a thousand sighs into the glass,
but none of them could dry the tears.
I smiled at you across the candle,
and even though you were not there,
I saw the shimmering sadness
flickering, deep inside your eyes.

you reached out and touched my hand,
and your eyes and your touch
were suddenly summer bright. Your
face burned with the radiance of a
thousand sunflecked kisses,
and as I softly reached for you,
you laughed and disappeared,
and I was once again alone.

You were not there, and though
I sat in front of the fire, I
froze... I wept... I paid... I left...

Tomorrow is one week.... an eternity.

No sleep came to claim my eyes last night,
just listless dreams,
relentlessly pursuing,
consuming my awakeness.
Every time I closed my eyes,
kaleidoscopes in weird disguise,
turning slowly,
like a giant wheel of fortune,
ever turning, never stopping,
pro and con the fusion,
hazy the illusion.

The wrong wind is blowing you around,
it fills your empty sails,
and crashes you aground...

The wrong ship is sheltered in your dock,
rotting in your harbor,
like a rusty, crowing cock...

Tainted with the purity of the ages
Stricken by the death of her depravity,
She decays there—a wasted saint—
withering in her whiteness.

Illumined by the light of her lost lust,
blinded by its lurid, Godly flame,
She descends to Heaven's deadly dust,
remembering not his name.

Sweet mercy's memory menopause
cannot exchange the cancers cause,
nor shroud-like shadows weave a sunbare shade.

No pallid, plastic, paisley eyes
can hide the blackened dawnless skies,
that rant and rage in silent thunder,
roaring soundless, endless wonder,
flogged by censured cravings hunger,
rotting in the pit of her reform...

Writheless marble mania, frozen
in the frantic fear of dawn.

(I was mad. My ex-wife tried to run me over with
the car. P.S. I deserved it.)

The flame of love, once lit,
becomes eternal if you feed it.
Like the candle's flame,
it must be tended, protected from
the violent winds of jealousy and
distrust.
It must be sheltered from
the rain and storms,
and, even when it seems to dim
and fade away,
you'll still find it there
glowing out of the darkness
lighting your way to forever

Keeper of the Flame

In some perfumed passion parlor,
with golden girls alive and baiting,
and black eyed beauties decked and fawning,
I await the crystal dawning.

On a bed of crimson flowers,
I spend groping, senseless hours,
drawing strength from poppied powers.
It's for you that I am waiting,
searching for your other face...
and a wisp of you comes seeping
to this voided, timeless place...

In the gray and yellow morning,
as I wake from never sleeping,
to my dazed and endless weeping,
I press closely to a stranger...

And her tender hands are torture,
and her kisses cannot save me
for they taste like watered wine,
and her love cannot erase you
from my mind...

For I know not where I'm winding,
on this carousel of wonder,
as I gaze across the ages,
and see you on all the pages

Continued...

of the worn out songs
that tired lovers sing...
And my heart keeps slowly breaking
as you chase some fading rainbow
across the barren spaces of my mind.

Now, on these early, misty mornings,
through afternoons of yearning, into
evenings of desire
I attend a trembling fire...
Yea, I am the man, the solitary keeper of the flame...

(After a divorce on an acid trip in Las Vegas)

She was like a summer song
that didn't last for very long,
but now that summer's
been and gone-
I still can hear her singing.

Over and Over

Once I was carefree, my heart was a rover,
and I only lived for the time,
taking, not leaving, and always believing,
that Love was a rumor, an out of tune rhyme.

Then, out of nowhere, she came and she found me
enraptured me, captured my soul,
and in the darkness, with her arms around me,
I became a believer, and Love was my goal.

And we flew to the moon, in the arms of each other,
two lovers in love with their song,
but I boasted, too soon, of the joys I discovered, and
while I was boasting, the song went all wrong.

Now over and over, her, her memory keeps
haunting me,
taunting me, luring me on,
onward to nowhere, endlessly searching, I
still can't believe that she really is gone,
but over and over, forever and after,
the laughter of her lingers on,
and all I can remember is her burning ember that
came with the sunset, and left with the dawn.

And here, before the endless, desperate sea,
I stand, a wasted beggar,
stranded on the shore,
above the tide,
free from its flowing,
always watching,
never going.

DEALING WITH IT

What a strange, unearthly place this
land, without your love, is ... How
early comes the nighttime now, in
the middle of the sunless day.
The clouds surround me without touching,
like some phantom feathers, blowing in a
windless wind,
not knowing which way they are going ...

I missed falling in love last spring, Now,
autumn is here, and there is no One,
Many ... but no One ...

You still are all around me,
though I cannot see your face.
My heart will not allow me yet,
the peace I seek and cannot find.
Maybe tomorrow
someone else will smile,
and wipe your memory from my mind...

Once Upon A Summer

Once upon a summer,
when I was very young
you held my hand and taught me songs
that I had never sung;
songs of sweet surrender,
songs of sheer delight,
words that echo tenderly
throughout the lonely night.
Now that autumn's over,
and winter chills me through,
my heart remembers,
once upon a summer,
and it misses you.

Baby, I Miss You

Baby, I miss you
you were a prayer for me,
always were there for me,
you made my life a paradise,
for all the world to see...
but that was long ago,
and it's all over now,
still, in the afterglow,
I see your face somehow...
and in the morning light...
and in the dark of night,
Baby, I miss you.

You were my everything,
just like a breath of spring,
you came along,
and taught my heart
a brand new song to sing...
but that was yesterday,
and yesterday is gone, and
here am I alone,
still waiting for the dawn...
and in the morning light,
and in the dark of night,
Baby, I miss you.

Continued...

Now it's all history
and you are gone from me
and I'm alone
out on my own
Just like every fool should be
but in the dark of night, and
in the morning light, Baby, I
miss you.

I miss you for all the reasons that I love you...
for all the seasons of my life that we're apart...
I miss you for all the childish laughter that
we shared, forever after, each time that you
looked into my heart...
I love you... for all the reasons that I miss you...

One by one the bridges burn, and
slowly crumble to the ground. One
by one the pages turn,
and chapters, yellowed by the sun,
dissolve before our very eyes. The
words have died
but not the deeds.

Inch by inch the heart returns
Strand by strand, the slender thread
that tied us to a tender past
has raveled now its very last
and parted like a thunder crash.

Lie by lie the truth has died, and
once beguiling lover's eyes
become a hiding place for pride.

I traveled many years today
in search of your enchanted echo,
and you linger through the autumn
of my memory, like a wisp of orange smoke,
embracing tender skies
in midnight ecstasy...

And where are you now, with
your golden, glowing face, and
your eyes alive with lies?

Who listens to your voice
whimpering in the darkness?

Where are the hands
that always reached out fast,
when something they received?

Where are they now,
those arms that strangled
with their hunger?
What have their unopened eyes perceived?

How dim your faded voice is, now...
How fast the sunrise mounts the stars,
and cries aloud from Kingdoms high,

I love you... but... I'm a little busy now...

There are too many rivers between us...
too many mountains to cross ...
too many miles of unfriendly highway,
and too many daydreams lost...

There are too many acres of memory,
too many forests aflame...
too many nights of sun-blinded sorrow,
and too many lovers to name...

I see you now through different eyes,
dulled by years of senseless lies,
shaded by the sorrow there...
Eyes through which
your beauty shines no more...

The Road to Nowhere

I see you in the shadows of my mind. The
neon lights are shining in your eyes.
The raindrops glisten in your perfumed hair,
and I am here, alone, and you are there...

I see you in the darkness of your room,
a strange, familiar place that I once knew.
No fire burns, the ashes have grown cold,
but I am still a child, and you are old...

We're here a while, and while away the time,
the time of love, that only lovers share. The
time for wasting time is over now,
the now's for one who needs someone to care...

One day you'll turn and find that I am gone,
faded from you, like the aging dawn,
and I shall die, and yet be born anew,
to travel love's road, with another you.

The road to nowhere's paved with broken hearts,
the hearts of fools, who would not see the danger.
The road to nowhere's traveled all alone,
or with some other, worn out, wasted stranger...

I see you in the shadows of my mind,
the neon lights have faded from your eyes,
and rain no longer glistens in your hair,
and I am here with love, and you are... where?

Some dreams are dreamed,
but never done.
Some songs are played,
but never sung.
Hearts that dance alone,
dance to the music
of the unsung songs,
and the unfinished dreams.

My song is born to be heard.
by all the lovers,
waiting by their silent streams
to wade into the water,
but are afraid, afraid, afraid:

And so,
if this is how it really has to be,
I'll say goodbye
to all the songs
we could have sung together,
and keep on searching
for the rest of me...
Somewhere... I'll find you....

And once again, in this enchanted place,
I reach into the darkness, across the years,
across the ocean, through the tears,
and find your hand
and feel your light,
and touch your face,
and span a new eternity
in one swift night,
and all the while that we embrace
there is no thought of what or when,
and only now is here again...

Forgive me hate,
for I sin against you daily,
each time I search the streets,
looking for "The face".
Each time I walk the avenue.
looking from heart to heart,
hoping to find one that
understands mine.

A million rainbows crowd my world,
each with a promise of some undiscovered spring.
Hungry hearts come searching here, for some new
love
that they can count on...

Another time...
Another place...
another version of your face.
Another dream that didn't fast...
another fragment of the past.
Another kiss that tasted warm...
another window in the storm.
Another ribbon rainbow gone.
Another fleeting glimpse at why...
Another shadow, singed by summertime...
Another icy winter sky.
Another daydream named Desire.

I walked on the pier today,
and saw two lovers, sitting
in a smart café.
They were holding hands,
and eating French fries...

I saw a model ship in a window.
I looked at some pearls
in a tiny boardwalk store,
and, as I watched. the sunset
blanket the harbor
with dusky light,
I didn't miss you at all,
but I cried
for the first time in years...

I Move Around

I walk along the silver sand
of love's forgotten wonderland,
my arm around the emptiness of you,
I search the shadows for a trace
of your remembered, glowing face, and
think of all the things we used to do, and
I move around, from town to town,
because I just can't seem to settle down...

I watch the magic morning skies,
and see the sunrise of your eyes,
and linger in your golden, summer light,
I listen to the gentle rain,
she's whispering your name again, but
your day keeps fading into night... and
I move around, from town to town,
because I just can't seem to settle down.

I sail the oceans of the past,
on windless waves of shattered glass, and
see you on some foggy phantom shore, but
when I try to reach that ground,
I find I just can't turn around,
and I sail the starless seas once more...

Continued...

*Now you ride another road, and carry someone
else's load,
you light some other's highway with your smile,
and as I walk the silver sand of
love's forgotten wonderland,
I'll keep you in my memory all the while...
And I move around, from town to town,
because I just can't seem to settle down...*

Looking for Your Eyes

Oh the years between have changed me,
and time has rearranged me,
and the songs we used to hear
have long been still...
but I remember love and laughter,
words of Now and Everafter, that
we sang one night
on our enchanted hill....
But you can't go back to where you've been before,
that time has come and gone,
still I search for you in every golden summer sunrise,
and each time I think I've found you,
when I put my arms around. you,
I find someone else just wearing your disguise,
and I keep on looking for your eyes.

Every morning I'm reminded
of the times I was blinded,
by a love so bright I couldn't even see.
Now when I try to find tomorrow, all
I find is pain and sorrow,
and a ghost of you that never sets me free,
But you can't go back to where you've been before,
that time has come and gone,
still I search for you in every golden summer sunrise,
and each time I think I've found you,
when I put my arms around you,
I find. someone else just wearing your disguise,
and I keep on looking for your eyes.

Love that dies while it is young,
stays always in the morning sun.
Love that dies when it is old,
more oft than not, dies from the cold,
but love that dies while in its youth,
more oft than not dies from the truth.

So save your weeping 'til you're old,
and dying from the freezing cold,
and all that's left to warm your years
are tattered veils of scattered tears.

Now dry your eyes and face the dawn,
and, maybe, when your mist is gone,
you'll see another shining light,
perhaps to guide you through the night.

La Dee Da

So now the dance has ended,
it's time to leave the floor.
That curtain has descended,
La Dee Da,
c'est la vie,
that's amor

She loved you for the moment,
it was a moment to adore,
but now that moment's over
La Dee Da,
c'est la vie,
that's amor

Once she vowed her love would last forever,
then she said forever was a bore.
So what?
You've got to get yourself together.
You've heard the lies of love before.

New music is beginning
so get back on the floor.
There's always one more inning
La Dee Da,
c'est la vie,
that's amor

The moral of the story is
a fact we can't ignore.

I never knew the morning sun
would rise if you were gone,
I thought the dew drops would desert
the early summer dawn.
I never knew the streams would run
like ribbons, through the air,
I thought they all would dry away
because you were not there.
But you are gone, and
all of this goes on...

I've looked before into the eyes of love, and
tasted lips that promised cherry wine. I've
seen the glow of summer fade
a dozen times, and more
and, still have left some blossoms on the vine.

I've known before this gentle summer rain
and held a hand, warmed by a blazing heart.
I've rambled down this country lane
a dozen times or more,
and never yet have fallen quite apart.

I want to taste the lips of love
Once more, before I die.
I want to drink the valleys up,
And drain the wells bone dry.
I want to ride that golden-crested
Wave, onto the shore,
And when the tide has ebbed away,
I'll still be wanting more.

I want to feel the breath of love
Once more upon my face.
I want to hear my heart's voice sing:
"This is the time and place."
I want to take love in my arms
And feel her tender glow, And
if I can take her with me, I
won't be afraid to go...

*I love you
for the memories
you left behind,
forever lighting
some dark corner
of my mind
that would be dark
and empty still,
if you had never shined.*

A World Full of Laughter

I lived, for a while
in a world full of laughter,
in the fair spring of love's changing clime...
I've slept in
the sea foamy, cloudy hereafter, in
the winter of love's frozen time.
I've traveled the rainbow
and ridden the wind,
and sailed on an ocean of gold.
I've pleased me some pleasures,
and sinned me some sins,
and I've been to the moon, so I'm told.

I've tasted the Honey,
and wasted the wine,
and soared on the wings of the dove,
and once, I remember
I lived like a King,
in a passionate palace of love.

I lived for awhile
in a world full of laughter,
in the autumn of what used to be,
and through all the lifetimes
of love's everafter,
the summer of her stays with me...

Summer's Child

Summer's Child was wild and free
a rolling stone, cast from the sea a
hungry wind caressing me
and I loved her.

She was young and warm and fair
She wore a rainbow in her hair on
her lips a blossom rare
and I cared.

Summer's Child, a golden thing,
the echo of enchanted spring,
a song of love for me to sing
when nights grow lonely.

Summertime has come and gone,
she glanced my way, then wandered on,
but Summer's Child will stay with me all
winter long ...

In Paradise

The day is almost done
and soon the setting sun
will kiss the sea goodnight.

It slowly slips away
and all at once the day
is fading out of sight.

We stand upon the shore
of life's forevermore -
remembering all we had.

The laughter and the fun,
the silly things we've done,
the good times, not the bad.

The summer rain, the silver moon, the
songs we hear when lovers croon.
Remembered dreams have all come true -
they've stayed alive inside of you .

And now we know so well
what only time will tell -
That lovers always last.

We've weathered every storm,
our hearts are safe and warm
not prisoners of the past .
And suddenly it's very clear,
we're meant to stay together dear
and love forevermore right here in paradise.

(The theme of Pau Hana Years PBS Honolulu, HI)

A Taste of Honey

Cold winds may blow o'er the icy sea But
I'll take with me the warmth of thee A
taste of honey
A taste much sweeter than wine

I will return I
will return
I'll come back
For the honey and you

I'll leave behind my heart to wear
And may it e'er remind you of
A taste of honey
A taste much sweeter than wine

I will return I
will return
I'll come back
For the honey and you

She tied his heart with her ribbon there
and felt his lips and his kiss so warm
His kiss was honey
A taste much sweeter than wine

Continued...

I will return I
will return
I'll come back
For the honey and you

He ne'er came back to his love so fair
and so she died
dreaming of his kiss
His kiss was honey
A taste more bitter than wine

I will return I
will return
I'll come back
For the honey and you

("A Taste of Honey" was written for the award-
winning play of the same name.)

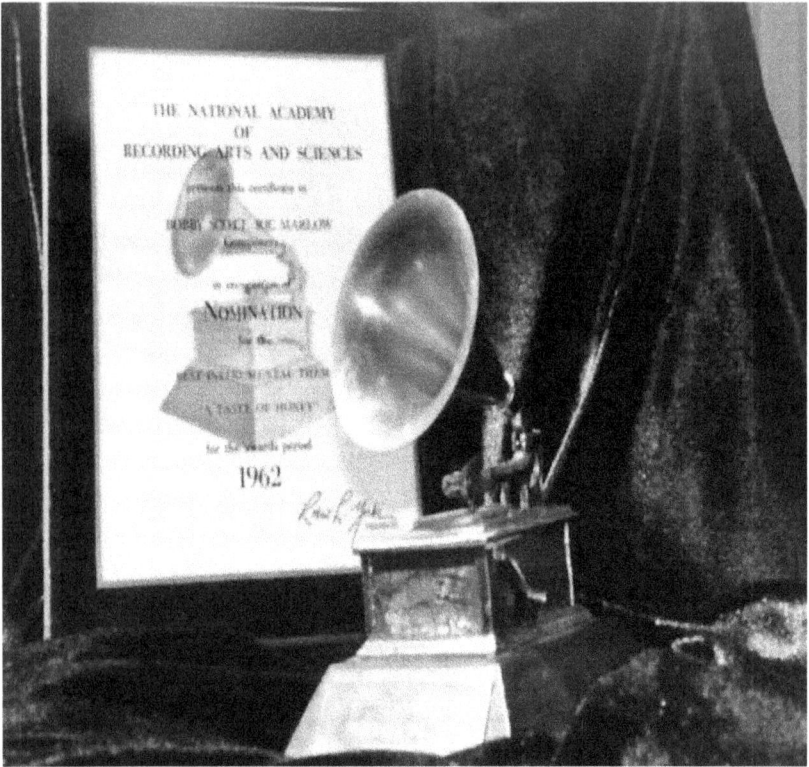

"A Taste of Honey" is one of the most commercially successful songs in the history of the music "business." It has been recorded by more than 150 international artists including The Beatles, Tony Bennett, Barbra Streisand, Morgana King, Herb Alpert and the Tijuana Brass, selling more than 300 million records and earning a Grammy for Ric Marlow. The song is still current today.

About the Author

Ric Marlow is the world's most extraordinary lyric talent! With the rare ability to express what he feels in an artistic, simple, and direct manner. Ric has created what every great performer looks for in his life: a vehicle through which to express the full range of emotions which make up the essence of what we call "our lives."

Ric's career has spanned decades in the entertainment business, but includes many interim jobs. Taxi cab driver, carpenter, police reporter, moving man, bread wrapper, fabric salesman, pogo stick demonstrator at Macy's toy department, etc. etc. etc. You name it, Ric has been there, done that, and done it well. Five wives. Many different lives. Many different passions. But he's still the same guy. ~ P. Valentino

www.ingramcontent.com/pod-product-compliance
Lightning Source LLC
Chambersburg PA
CBHW061748020426
42331CB00006B/1392